FAITH

POPE BENEDICT XVI

SPIRITUAL THOUGHTS SERIES

Edited by and preface by Lucio Coco

United States Conference of Catholic Bishops
Washington, DC

First printing, February 2013
ISBN 978-1-60137-374-8

CONTENTS

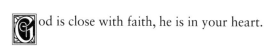od is close with faith, he is in your heart.

BENEDICT XVI

INTRODUCTION

In the fall of 2011, on the occasion of the Eucharistic celebration at the conclusion of the first international encounter sponsored by the Pontifical Council for the Promotion of the New Evangelization, Pope Benedict XVI announced the inauguration of a "Year of Faith," to run from October 11, 2012, the fiftieth anniversary of the opening of the Second Vatican Council, until November 24, 2013, the Solemnity of Christ the King, the conclusion of the liturgical year. On that occasion, the Holy Father himself summarized the motivation that led him to promote such an event: "To give a fresh impetus to the mission of the whole Church to lead human beings out of the wilderness in which they often find themselves" (Homily, October 16, 2011). He added that the goal of the Year of Faith is to show people Christ and the way to grow in friendship with him. In this vein, he repeated the words that expressed his own program as pope, which he had also pronounced in the inaugural homily of his Petrine ministry: "The Church as a whole and all her Pastors, like Christ, must set out to lead people out of the desert, toward the place of life, toward friendship with the Son of God, toward the One who gives us life, and life in abundance" (Homily, April 24, 2005).

The Holy Father returns to this passage again in the Apostolic Letter in the form of a motu proprio to open the Year of Faith (cf. Apostolic Letter *Porta Fidei*, no. 2), and in the *Angelus* that followed the Mass for the New Evangelization, he reiterates the importance of recalling "the beauty and centrality of faith, the need to reinforce it and to deepen it at the personal and the community level" (*Angelus*, October 16, 2011), and calls for living out the Year of Faith "in a perspective that is . . . missionary, with a view precisely to the mission *ad gentes* and the New Evangelization" (ibid.). The pontificate of Pope Benedict XVI likewise exemplifies concretely what he proposes programmatically: bringing Christ to men, making his word of salvation known to people of the twenty-first century, proclaiming it to those who are far off, not so much and not only those who are materially or geographically distant but rather those who, even though they are close to the sources of the faith, inhabit the spiritual desert typical of a modernity that has renounced God. It is not by chance that the word "desert" recurs frequently in the Holy Father's speeches to point out just this no-man's-land of extreme aridity where God and Christ are sidelined and man sinks unavoidably into an existential solitude, with values that actually torture the spirit.

In the pope's words, there is also a warning not to make the Year of Faith "a celebration" (cf. *Angelus*, October 16, 2011). Everything can be celebrated except faith. As can be seen from many thoughts present in this collection, Pope Benedict XVI teaches us that faith is a foundational act of the person. By means of faith, I make decisions about myself and my truth every time, not only when I show myself to measure up to the teachings of Christ, but also when I break them out of weakness and frailty and I choose the non-faith of someone who does not know how to make the leap forward from himself toward God.

Faith is always openness, a renunciation of the occasionally arrogant traits of the ego and the choice to trust in God, to recommit to his will, to surrender to his providence, to become open to receive his grace. In his interventions, the Holy Father sounds a constant call to make room for God in our life, to entrust ourselves to him, to seek him in the difficult and sad moments of existence and to listen to his Word when we are called upon to choose between the good and evil that life sets before us every day, and when maintaining our integrity is itself an act of faith, because everything cannot be indifferent and relative, everything cannot pass by unnoticed, and my good act and my sin cannot have the same weight.

This is what the Year of Faith wishes to remind us of continually from today on: the fact that in every moment we are called to go beyond ourselves and toward God in our actions and decisions; not to let ourselves be shaped by indifference and to open our hearts to the wide horizon of a Transcendence that is charity and that cares for us. Pope Benedict wants to bring us back to this ideal of faith just as he has done since his election as pope. It is up to us to seize this latest occasion offered to us and to make this Year a year of grace to attain to an experience of faith as "a lifelong companion that makes it possible to perceive, ever anew, the marvels that God works for us" (*Porta Fidei*, no. 15).

Lucio Coco

FAITH

The "door of faith" (Acts 14:27) is always open for us, ushering us into the life of communion with God and offering entry into his Church. It is possible to cross that threshold when the word of God is proclaimed and the heart allows itself to be shaped by transforming grace.

PORTA FIDEI, NO. 1
OCTOBER 11, 2011

I. THE GIFT OF FAITH

1. *On the initiative of God*

Faith is not the result of human effort, of human reasoning, but rather a gift of God: "Blessed are you, Simon son of Jonah! For flesh and blood has not revealed this to you, but my Father in heaven." Faith starts with God, who opens his heart to us and invites us to share in his own divine life.

Homily at Mass for World Youth Day
August 21, 2011

2. *Grace and gift*

Faith, understood as a fruit of the experience of God's love, is a grace, a gift of God. Yet human beings will only be able to experience faith as a grace to the extent that they accept it within themselves as a gift on which they seek to live.

Letter on the 50th anniversary of Haurietis Aquas
May 15, 2006

3. *Gift and grace*

The heart indicates that the first act by which one comes to faith is God's gift and the action of grace which acts and transforms the person deep within.

Porta Fidei, no. 10
October 11, 2011

4. *Already and not yet*

Faith is not merely a personal reaching out toward things to come that are still totally absent: it gives us something. It gives us even now something of the reality we are waiting for, and this present reality constitutes for us a "proof" of the things that are still unseen. Faith draws the future into the present, so that it is no longer simply a "not yet." The fact that this future exists changes the present; the present is touched by the future reality, and thus the things of the future spill over into those of the present and those of the present into those of the future.

Encylical On Christian Hope *(*Spe Salvi*)*
November 30, 2007

5. *Perspective*

Faith is not merely the attachment to a complex of dogmas, complete in itself, that is supposed to satisfy the thirst for God, present in the human heart. On the contrary, it guides human beings on their way through time toward a God who is ever new in his infinity.

Angelus
August 28, 2005

6. *Closeness*

God is close with faith, he is in your heart, and with confession he is on your lips. He is within you and with you.

Reflection for the special assembly of African bishops
October 5, 2009

7. *Conditions*

Faith, ultimately, is a gift. Consequently, the first condition is to let ourselves be given something, not to be self-sufficient or do everything by ourselves—because we cannot—but to open ourselves in the awareness that the Lord truly gives.

Meeting with clergy of the Diocese of Rome
March 2, 2006

8. *Working of grace*

Faith, then, is not merely a cultural heritage, but the constant working of the grace of God who calls and our human freedom, which can respond or not to his call.

Homily at Mass in Valencia, Spain
July 9, 2006

9. *Openness*

Faith thus entails the opening of the person to the Lord's grace; it means recognizing that everything is a gift, everything is grace. What a treasure is hidden in two small words: "thank you!"

Angelus
October 14, 2007

II. FAITH IN JESUS

The Christian faith is first and foremost the encounter with Jesus.

GENERAL AUDIENCE
OCTOBER 3, 2007

10. *Newness and oneness*

Faith opens us to knowing and welcoming the real identity of Jesus, his newness and oneness, his word, as a source of life, in order to live a personal relationship with him.

Angelus
August 14, 2011

11. *Relationship*

Faith is more than the mere acceptance of certain abstract truths: it is an intimate relationship with Christ, who enables us to open our hearts to this mystery of love and to live as men and women conscious of being loved by God.

Homily at prayer vigil for World Youth Day
August 20, 2011

12. *Surrender*

Faith does not simply provide information about who Christ is; rather, it entails a personal relationship with Christ, a surrender of our whole person, with all our understanding, will and feelings, to God's self-revelation.

Homily at Mass for World Youth Day
August 21, 2011

13. *Faith and discipleship*

Faith in Christ and discipleship are strictly interconnected. And, since faith involves following the Master, it must become constantly stronger, deeper and more mature, to the extent that it leads to a closer and more intense relationship with Jesus.

Homily at Mass for World Youth Day
August 21, 2011

14. *To believe*

Faith is not a theory. To believe is to enter into a personal relationship with Jesus and to live in friendship with him in fellowship with others, in the communion of the Church. Entrust the whole of your lives to Christ and bring your friends to find their way to the source of life, to God. May the Lord make you happy and joy-filled witnesses of his love.

Angelus
August 21, 2011

15. *Faith in a Person*

Knowledge of the faith grows; it grows with the desire to find the way and in the end it is a gift of God who does not reveal himself to us as an abstract thing without a face or a name, because faith responds to a Person who wants to enter into a relationship of deep love with us and to involve our whole life.

Angelus
August 14, 2011

16. *Duty*

Faith does not just mean accepting a certain number of abstract truths about the mysteries of God, of man, of life and death, of future realities. Faith consists in an intimate relationship with Christ, a relationship based on love of him who loved us first (cf. 1 Jn 4:11), even to the total offering of himself.

Homily at Mass in Warsaw, Poland
May 26, 2006

17. *Encounter*

Faith is first and foremost a personal, intimate encounter with Jesus, it is having an experience of his closeness, his friendship and his love. It is in this way that we learn to know him ever better, to love him and to follow him more and more.

General audience
October 21, 2009

18. *Mystical union*

Although faith unites us closely to Christ, it emphasizes the distinction between us and him; but according to Paul, Christian life also has an element that we might describe as "mystical," since it entails an identification of ourselves with Christ and of Christ with us.

General audience
November 8, 2006

19. *"Give us faith"*

We too are called to grow in faith, to open ourselves in order to welcome God's gift freely, to have trust and also to cry to Jesus, "Give us faith, help us to find the way!"

Angelus
August 14, 2011

20. *Keywords*

Faith is a journey led by the Holy Spirit which can be summed up in two words: conversion and discipleship.

Meeting with the bishops of Brazil
May 11, 2007

21. *Unity in faith*

Our common effort on the way toward full unity is essential, but let us always be well aware that we ourselves can "make" neither faith nor the unity we so deeply long for.

A faith created by ourselves has no value, and true unity is indeed a gift of the Lord, who always prayed and still prays for the unity of his disciples. Christ alone can bestow this unity upon us and we will be ever more united to the extent that we turn to him and let ourselves be transformed by him.

General audience
September 28, 2011

22. *The Year of Faith*

The Year of Faith . . . is a summons to an authentic and renewed conversion to the Lord, the one Savior of the world. In the mystery of his death and resurrection, God has revealed in its fullness the Love that saves and calls us to conversion of life through the forgiveness of sins (cf. Acts 5:31).

Porta Fidei, no. 6
October 11, 2011

III. TOTAL ENTRUSTMENT TO GOD

Faith in God defends man in all his frailty and shortcomings.

HOMILY AT MASS FOR THE ORDINATION OF NEW BISHOPS
SEPTEMBER 29, 2007

23. *Surrendering ourselves*

Believing means surrendering ourselves to God and entrusting our destiny to him. Believing means entering into a personal relationship with our Creator and Redeemer in the power of the Holy Spirit, and making this relationship the basis of our whole life.

*Homily at Mass in Krakow, Poland
May 28, 2006*

24. *Certitude*

Only through believing, then, does faith grow and become stronger; there is no other possibility for possessing certitude with regard to one's life apart from self-abandonment, in a continuous crescendo, into the hands of a love that seems to grow constantly because it has its origin in God.

Porta Fidei, no. 7
October 11, 2011

25. *The troubled faith of Peter*

Peter walks on the water, not by his own effort but rather through divine grace in which he believes. And when he was smitten by doubt, when he no longer fixed his gaze on Jesus but was frightened by the gale, when he failed to put full trust in the Teacher's words, it means that he was interiorly distancing himself from the Teacher and so risked sinking in the sea of life. So it is also for us: if we look only at ourselves we become dependent on the winds and can no longer pass through storms on the waters of life.

Angelus
August 7, 2011

26. *Losing faith*

This is the extreme temptation to which the believer is subjected, the temptation to lose faith, to lose trust in God's closeness. The righteous pass the final test, remain steadfast in faith, in the certainty of the truth and in full trust in God; in this way they find life and truth.

General audience
September 7, 2011

27. Disbelief

Beset by many problems we are tempted to think that perhaps God does not save me, that he does not know me, perhaps he is not able to; the temptation to lose faith is our enemy's ultimate attack and if we are to find God, if we are to find life, we must resist it.

General audience
September 7, 2011

28. Dark nights

When we enter the terrain of faith, in the "land of faith," we often encounter a dark and difficult life, a sowing in tears, but we are confident that the light of Christ will really grant us a great harvest in the end. In the dark nights we also need to learn this: not to forget that there is a light, that God is already in the midst of our life and that we can sow with great trust that God's "yes" is stronger than us all. It is important not to lose this memory of God's presence in our life, this profound joy that God has entered into our life and set us free. This is gratitude for finding Jesus Christ who has come to us. And this gratitude is transformed into hope, it is a star of hope that gives us reason to trust; it is light, because the very pains of the sowing are the beginning of the new life, of the great and definitive joy of God.

General audience
October 12, 2011

29. *In trial*

When we face the most difficult and painful situations, when it seems that God does not hear, we must not be afraid to entrust the whole weight of our overburdened hearts to him, we must not fear to cry out to him in our suffering, we must be convinced that God is close, even if he seems silent.

General audience
February 8, 2012

30. *The way*

Faith can always bring us back to God even when our sin leads us astray.

Address to men and women religious,
Częstochowa, Poland
May 26, 2006

31. *Faith and prayer*

The power that changes the world and transforms it into the Kingdom of God, in silence and without fanfare, is faith—and prayer is the expression of faith.

Homily at Mass in Naples, Italy
October 21, 2007

32. *In the love of God*

Even in the face of death, faith can make possible what is humanly impossible. But faith in what? In the love of God. This is the real answer which radically defeats Evil. Just as Jesus confronted the Evil One with the power of the love that came to him from the Father, so we too can confront and live through [trials] . . . , keeping our heart immersed in God's love.

Angelus
February 5, 2012

33. *Prayer*

May the Lord give us faith,
may he come to our aid in our weakness
and make us capable of believing
and praying in every anxiety,
in the sorrowful nights of doubt
and the long days of sorrow,
abandoning ourselves with trust to him,
who is our "shield" and our "glory."

General audience
September 7, 2011

IV. BELIEVING WITH THE CHURCH

The Church's mission is always nourished by the faith and hope of the Christian people.

HOMILY AT MASS IN NAPLES, ITALY
OCTOBER 21, 2007

34. *Believing with*

Faith always includes as an essential element the fact that it is shared with others. No one can believe alone. We receive the faith—as St. Paul tells us—through hearing, and hearing is part of being together, in spirit and in body. Only within this great assembly of believers of all times, who found Christ and were found by him, am I able to believe. In the first place I have God to thank for the fact that I can believe, for God approaches me and so to speak "ignites" my faith. But on a practical level, I have my fellow human beings to thank for my faith, those who believed before me and who believe with me. This great "with," apart from which there can be no personal faith, is the Church.

Homily at Mass in Erfurt, Germany
September 24, 2011

35. *Letting ourselves fall*

No one believes purely on his own. We always believe in and with the Church. The Creed is always a shared act, it means letting ourselves be incorporated into a communion of progress, life, words and thought. We do not "have" faith, in the sense that it is primarily God who gives it to us. Nor do we "have" it either, in the sense that it must not be invented by us. We must let ourselves fall, so to speak, into the communion of faith, of the Church. Believing is in itself a Catholic act. It is participation in this great certainty, which is present in the Church as a living subject.

Meeting with clergy of the Diocese of Rome
March 2, 2006

36. *Born in the faith*

Having faith means drawing support from the faith of your brothers and sisters, even as your own faith serves as a support for the faith of others. I ask you, dear friends, to love the Church which brought you to birth in the faith, which helped you to grow in the knowledge of Christ and which led you to discover the beauty of his love. Growing in friendship with Christ necessarily means recognizing the importance of joyful participation in the life of your parishes, communities and movements, as well as the celebration of Sunday Mass, frequent reception of the sacrament of Reconciliation, and the cultivation of personal prayer and meditation on God's word.

Homily at Mass for World Youth Day
August 21, 2011

37. *In the communion of the Church*

Following Jesus in faith means walking at his side in the communion of the Church. We cannot follow Jesus on our own. Anyone who would be tempted to do so "on his own," or to approach the life of faith with that kind of individualism so prevalent today, will risk never truly encountering Jesus, or will end up following a counterfeit Jesus.

Homily at Mass for World Youth Day
August 21, 2011

38. *Relationship*

The Christian faith is not something purely spiritual and internal, nor is our relationship with Christ itself exclusively subjective and private. Rather, it is a completely concrete and ecclesial relationship.

Meeting with clergy of the Diocese of Rome
May 13, 2005

39. *Counteraction*

With her long tradition of respect for the right relationship between faith and reason, the Church has a critical role to play in countering cultural currents which, on the basis of an extreme individualism, seek to promote notions of freedom detached from moral truth. Our tradition does not speak from blind faith, but from a rational perspective which links our commitment to building an authentically just, humane and prosperous society to our ultimate assurance that the cosmos is possessed of an inner logic accessible to human reasoning.

Meeting with the bishops of the United States
January 19, 2012

40. *Like Mary*

[Mary] welcomed Jesus with faith and gave him to the world with love. This is also our vocation and our mission, the vocation and mission of the Church: to welcome Christ into our lives and give him to the world, so "that the world might be saved through him" (Jn 3:17).

Angelus
December 8, 2006

V. EDUCATION IN THE FAITH

Education in the faith must first of all consist in developing all that is good in the human being.

ADDRESS TO THE BISHOPS OF POLAND
NOVEMBER 26, 2005

41. *Fides ex auditu*

Faith, as knowledge and profession of the truth about God and about man, "comes from what is heard, and what is heard comes by the preaching of Christ," as St. Paul says (Rom 10:17).

Homily at Mass in Warsaw, Poland
May 26, 2006

42. *Discovery*

Discovering the beauty and joy of faith is a path that every new generation must take on its own, for all that we have that is most our own and most intimate is staked on faith:

our heart, our mind, our freedom, in a deeply personal relationship with the Lord at work within us.

Address to the ecclesial convention of the
Diocese of Rome
June 5, 2006

43. *Questions*

First of all, we have to ask questions. Those who do not ask do not get a reply. But I would add that for theology, in addition to the courage to ask, we also need the humility to listen to the answers that the Christian faith gives us.

Address to theology faculty at
University of Tübingen, Germany
March 21, 2007

44. *The witness*

The central figure in the work of educating, and especially in education in the faith, which is the summit of the person's formation and is his or her most appropriate horizon, is specifically the form of witness. This witness becomes a proper reference point to the extent that the person can account for the hope that nourishes his life (cf. 1 Pt 3:15) and is personally involved in the truth that he proposes. On the other hand, the witness never refers to himself but to something, or rather, to Someone greater than he, whom he has encountered and whose dependable goodness he has sampled. Thus, every educator and witness finds an unequalled model in Jesus Christ, the Father's great witness, who said nothing about himself but spoke as the Father had taught him (cf. Jn 8:28).

Address to participants in the ecclesial diocesan
convention of Rome
June 6, 2005

45. *Crisis of faith* (1)

As we know, in vast areas of the earth faith risks being extinguished, like a flame that is no longer fed. We are facing a profound crisis of faith, a loss of the religious sense that constitutes the greatest challenge to the Church today. The renewal of faith must therefore take priority in the commitment of the entire Church in our time. I hope that the Year of Faith will contribute, with the cordial cooperation of all the members of the People of God, to making God present in this world once again and to giving men and women access to the faith to entrust themselves to the God who loved us to the very end (cf. Jn 13:1), in Jesus Christ, Crucified and Risen.

Address to the Congregation for the
Doctrine of the Faith
January 27, 2012

46. *Crisis of faith* (2)

It often happens that Christians are more concerned for the social, cultural and political consequences of their commitment, continuing to think of the faith as a self-evident presupposition for life in society. In reality, not only can this presupposition no longer be taken for granted, but it is often openly denied. Whereas in the past it was possible to recognize a unitary cultural matrix, broadly accepted in its appeal to the content of the faith and the values inspired by it, today this no longer seems to be the case in large swathes of society, because of a profound crisis of faith that has affected many people.

Porta Fidei, no. 2
October 11, 2011

47. *Joy*

To the extent that we nourish ourselves on Christ and are in love with him, we feel within us the incentive to bring others to him: indeed, we cannot keep the joy of the faith to ourselves; we must pass it on. This need becomes even stronger and more pressing in the context of that strange forgetfulness of God which has spread in vast areas of the world today. . . . This forgetfulness is giving rise to a lot of fleeting chatter, to many useless arguments, but also to great dissatisfaction and a sense of emptiness.

Address to the ecclesial convention of the
Diocese of Rome
June 5, 2006

48. *Proclamation*

We must return to proclaiming powerfully and joyfully the event of Christ's death and Resurrection, heart of Christianity, principal fulcrum of our faith, powerful lever of our certainty, impetuous wind that sweeps away every fear and indecision, every doubt and human calculation. This decisive change in the world can only come from God.

Homily at Mass in Verona, Italy
October 19, 2006

49. *Faith in the Word*

Only if each one of the faithful allows his or her personal and community life to be joined to the Word of Christ, who asks for a personal and adult response of faith through authentic and lasting conversion with a view to social fruitfulness and brotherhood among all, can the Gospel profoundly illumine their consciences and transform cultures from within.

Meeting with the bishops of the Congo
January 27, 2006

50. *Putting the Word into practice*

The Christian's life is a life of faith, founded on the Word of God and nourished by it. In the trials of life and in every temptation, the secret of victory lies in listening to the Word of truth and rejecting with determination falsehood and evil. This is the true and central program of the [Christian]: to listen to the word of truth, to live, speak and do what is true, to refuse falsehood that poisons humanity and is the vehicle of all evils.

General audience
March 1, 2006

51. *To young people*

The first point is *the proclamation of the faith to the youth of our time.* Young people today live in a secularized culture, totally oriented to material things. In daily life—in the means of communication, at work, in leisure time—they experience at most a culture in which God is absent. Yet, they are waiting for God.

Meeting with bishops of Germany
November 18, 2006

52. *The Christian family*

The Christian family passes on the faith when parents teach their children to pray and when they pray with them (cf. *Familiaris Consortio*, no. 60); when they lead them to the sacraments and gradually introduce them to the life of the Church; when all join in reading the Bible, letting the light of faith shine on their family life and praising God as our Father.

Homily at Mass in Valencia, Spain
July 9, 2006

53. *Domestic Church*

The language of faith is learned in homes where this faith grows and is strengthened through prayer and Christian practice.

Address to families in Valencia, Spain
July 8, 2006

54. *The certainty of faith*

Unless we learn anew the foundations of life—unless we discover in a new way the certainty of faith—it will be less and less possible for us to entrust to others the gift of life and the task of an unknown future.

Address to the members of the Roman Curia
December 22, 2006

55. *The* Catechism of the Catholic Church

The Year of Faith will have to see a concerted effort to rediscover and study the fundamental content of the faith that receives its systematic and organic synthesis in the *Catechism of the Catholic Church.*

Porta Fidei, no. 11
October 11, 2011

VI. FAITH AND THEOLOGICAL VIRTUES

[Faith] is the lifelong companion that makes it possible to perceive, ever anew, the marvels that God works for us.

PORTA FIDEI, NO. 15
OCTOBER 11, 2011

1. Faith and Hope

56. *Antidote*

Faith, which is active in charity, is the true antidote against a nihilistic mentality that is spreading its influence in the world even more in our time.

Angelus
November 18, 2007

57. *Substance*

Faith is the substance of hope.

> Spe Salvi, *no. 10*
> *November 30, 2007*

58. *Crisis*

The present-day crisis of faith . . . is essentially a crisis of Christian hope.

> Spe Salvi, *no. 17*
> *November 30, 2007*

59. *Anchor*

Christian hope, rooted in a firm faith in the word of Christ, is the anchor of salvation that helps us overcome seemingly insurmountable difficulties and makes it possible for us to catch a glimpse of the light of joy beyond the darkness of pain and death.

> *Homily at the funeral Mass for Cardinal Dino Monduzzi*
> *October 16, 2006*

2. Faith and Love

60. *Path*

Faith is a journey of illumination: it starts with the humility of recognizing oneself as needy of salvation and arrives at the personal encounter with Christ, who calls one to follow him on the way of love.

Angelus
October 29, 2006

61. *Thirst*

God thirsts for our faith and our love.

Angelus
February 24, 2008

62. *Experience of love*

Faith grows when it is lived as an experience of love received and when it is communicated as an experience of grace and joy.

Porta Fidei, *no. 7*
October 11, 2011

63. *Reciprocity*

Faith without charity bears no fruit, while charity without faith would be a sentiment constantly at the mercy of doubt. Faith and charity each require the other, in such a way that each allows the other to set out along its respective path.

Porta Fidei, *no. 14*
October 11, 2011

64. *The faith of Christians*

[St. Paul] wrote in his Letter to the Romans: "We hold that a man is justified by faith apart from works of law" (3:28). . . . Paul states with absolute clarity that this condition of life does not depend on our possible good works but on the pure grace of God: "[We] are justified by his grace as a gift, through the redemption which is in Christ Jesus" (Rom 3:24).

General audience
November 8, 2006

VII. FAITH AND REASON

Faith has a rational and intellectual dimension of its own which is essential to it.

ADDRESS TO STUDENTS AND TEACHERS OF
ALMO COLLEGIO CAPRANICA
JANUARY 20, 2012

65. A reasonable faith

We must be people who live faith and think faith, people with an inner knowledge of it. So it is that faith becomes reason within us, it becomes reasonable.

*Meeting with the clergy of the Dioceses of
Belluno-Feltre and Treviso
September 24, 2007*

66. Reciprocity

God truly enters into human affairs only when, rather than being present merely in our thinking, he himself comes toward us and speaks to us. Reason therefore needs faith if it is to be completely itself: reason and faith need one another in order to fulfill their true nature and their mission.

Spe Salvi, *no. 23*
November 30, 2007

67. *Natural friendship*

A natural friendship exists between faith and reason, founded in the order of Creation itself. In the *incipit* of the Encyclical *Fides et Ratio*, the Servant of God John Paul II wrote: "Faith and reason are like two wings on which the human spirit rises to the contemplation of truth." Faith is open to the effort of understanding by reason; reason, in turn, recognizes that faith does not mortify her but on the contrary impels her towards vaster and loftier horizons. The eternal lesson of monastic theology fits in here. Faith and reason, in reciprocal dialogue, are vibrant with joy when they are both inspired by the search for intimate union with God.

General audience
October 28, 2009

68. *Acceptance*

To believe means first to accept as true what our mind cannot fully comprehend. We have to accept what God reveals to us about himself, about ourselves, about everything around us, including the things that are invisible, inexpressible and beyond our imagination. This act of accepting revealed truth broadens the horizon of our knowledge and draws us to the mystery in which our lives are immersed. Letting our reason be limited in this way is not something easy to do. Here we see the second aspect of faith: it is trust in a person, no ordinary person, but Jesus Christ himself. What we believe is important, but even more important is the One in whom we believe.

Homily at Mass in Krakow, Poland
May 28, 2006

69. *Preamble*

We must not forget that in our cultural context, very many people, while not claiming to have the gift of faith, are nevertheless sincerely searching for the ultimate meaning and definitive truth of their lives and of the world. This search is an authentic "preamble" to the faith, because it guides people onto the path that leads to the mystery of God. Human reason, in fact, bears within itself a demand for "what is perennially valid and lasting." This demand constitutes a permanent summons, indelibly written into the human heart, to set out to find the One whom we would not be seeking had he not already set out to meet us. To this encounter, faith invites us and it opens us in fullness.

Porta Fidei, no. 10
October 11, 2011

70. *Perspectives*

Faith, in fact, can offer perspectives of hope to every project that has human destiny at its core. Faith examines the invisible and is thus a friend of reason, which asks itself the essential questions from which it draws meaning for our earthly journey.

Address to members of lay associations
November 11, 2006

VIII. WITNESS TO FAITH

A Christian may never think of belief as a private act.

PORTA FIDEI, NO. 10
OCTOBER 11, 2011

71. *Premise*

Prescinding from God, acting as if he did not exist or relegating faith to the purely private sphere, undermines the truth about man and compromises the future of culture and society. On the contrary, lifting one's gaze to the living God, the guarantor of our freedom and of truth, is a premise for arriving at a new humanity.

Letter to the bishops of Spain
July 8, 2006

72. *Consistency*

Faith cannot be reduced to a private sentiment or indeed, be hidden when it is inconvenient; it also implies consistency and a witness even in the public arena for the sake of human beings, justice and truth.

Angelus
October 9, 2005

73. *Openness*

Knowing the content to be believed is not sufficient unless the heart, the authentic sacred space within the person, is opened by grace that allows the eyes to see below the surface and to understand that what has been proclaimed is the word of God.

Porta Fidei, *no. 10*
October 11, 2011

74. *Standing with the Lord*

Faith is choosing to stand with the Lord so as to live with him. This "standing with him" points toward an understanding of the reasons for believing. Faith, precisely because it is a free act, also demands social responsibility for what one believes.

Porta Fidei, *no. 10*
October 11, 2011

75. Generosity

God likes to carry out his works using poor means. He therefore asks you to make a generous faith available to him!

Address to charitable organizations
March 17, 2007

76. Witness to faith

The presence of faith in the world is a positive element, even if it does not convert anyone; it is a reference point.

Meeting with the clergy of the Diocese of Rome
February 7, 2008

77. Light

Only if a human being finds the light that illuminates him and offers him the fullness of meaning is he truly happy. This light is faith in Christ, the gift received in Baptism that must be constantly rediscovered if it is to be passed on to others.

Address at Sant'Antonio Parish, Concesio, Italy
November 8, 2009

78. Trial

In life's difficulties it is especially the quality of the faith of each one of us that is tried and tested: its firmness, its purity, its consistency with life.

Homily at Mass for the first anniversary of
Blessed John Paul II's death
April 3, 2006

79. *School*

The school of faith is not a triumphal march but a journey marked daily by suffering and love, trials and faithfulness.

General audience
May 24, 2006

80. *Living faith*

A strong faith must endure tests. A living faith must always grow. Our faith in Jesus Christ, to be such, must frequently face others' lack of faith.

Meeting with young people in Krakow, Poland
May 27, 2006

81. *True faith*

Faith [is] a fundamental attitude of the spirit, not merely something intellectual or sentimental; true faith involves the entire person: thoughts, affections, intentions, relations, bodiliness, activity and daily work.

General audience
May 31, 2006

82. *"Your faith has saved you"*

"*Fides tua te salvum fecit,*" the Lord said over and over again to those he healed. It was not the physical touch, it was not the external gesture that was operative, but the fact that those sick people believed. And we too can only serve the Lord energetically if our faith thrives and is present in abundance.

Address to the bishops of Switzerland
November 7, 2006

83. *Criterion*

Faith is not a theory that can be personalized or even set aside. It is something very concrete: it is the criterion that determines our lifestyle.

Address to the pontifical council "Cor Unum"
January 23, 2006

84. *The teaching of Mary*

Mary thus stands before us as a sign of comfort, encouragement and hope. She turns to us, saying: "Have the courage to dare with God! Try it! Do not be afraid of him! Have the courage to risk with faith! Have the courage to risk with goodness! Have the courage to risk with a pure heart! Commit yourselves to God, then you will see that it is precisely by doing so that your life will become broad and light, not boring but filled with infinite surprises, for God's infinite goodness is never depleted!"

Homily at Mass in St. Peter's Square
December 8, 2005

85. *Prayer*

Let us ask the Mother of God to obtain for us the gift of a mature faith: a faith that we would like to resemble hers as far as possible, a clear, genuine, humble and at the same time courageous faith, steeped in hope and enthusiasm for the Kingdom of God, a faith devoid of all fatalism and wholly set on cooperating with the divine will in full and joyful obedience and with the absolute certainty that God wants nothing but love and life, always and for everyone. Obtain for us, O Mary, an authentic, pure faith. May you always be thanked and blessed, Holy Mother of God! Amen!

Homily at Vespers and Te Deum
December 31, 2006

IX. THE HISTORY OF OUR FAITH

By faith, we too live: by the living recognition of the Lord Jesus, present in our lives and in our history.

PORTA FIDEI, NO. 13
OCTOBER 11, 2011

86. *Mary*

By faith, Mary accepted the Angel's word and believed the message that she was to become the Mother of God in the obedience of her devotion (cf. Lk 1:38). Visiting Elizabeth, she raised her hymn of praise to the Most High for the marvels he worked in those who trust him (cf. Lk 1:46-55). With joy and trepidation she gave birth to her only son, keeping her virginity intact (cf. Lk 2:6-7). Trusting in Joseph, her husband, she took Jesus to Egypt to save him from Herod's persecution (cf. Mt 2:13-15). With the same faith, she followed the Lord in his preaching and remained with him all the way to Golgotha (cf. Jn 19:25-27). By faith, Mary tasted the fruits of Jesus' resurrection, and treasuring every memory in her heart (cf. Lk 2:19, 51), she passed

them on to the Twelve assembled with her in the Upper
Room to receive the Holy Spirit (cf. Acts 1:14; 2:1-4).

Porta Fidei, *no. 13*
October 11, 2011

87. *The Apostles*

By faith, the Apostles left everything to follow their Master
(cf. Mk 10:28). They believed the words with which he
proclaimed the Kingdom of God present and fulfilled in
his person (cf. Lk 11:20). They lived in communion of life
with Jesus who instructed them with his teaching, leaving
them a new rule of life, by which they would be recognized
as his disciples after his death (cf. Jn 13:34-35). By faith,
they went out to the whole world, following the command
to bring the Gospel to all creation (cf. Mk 16:15) and they
fearlessly proclaimed to all the joy of the resurrection, of
which they were faithful witnesses.

Porta Fidei, *no. 13*
October 11, 2011

88. *The disciples*

By faith, the disciples formed the first community, gathered
around the teaching of the Apostles, in prayer, in celebration of the Eucharist, holding their possessions in common
so as to meet the needs of the brethren (cf. Acts 2:42-47).

Porta Fidei, *no. 13*
October 11, 2011

89. *The martyrs*

By faith, the martyrs gave their lives, bearing witness to the truth of the Gospel that had transformed them and made them capable of attaining to the greatest gift of love: the forgiveness of their persecutors.

Porta Fidei, no. 13
October 11, 2011

90. *Religious*

By faith, men and women have consecrated their lives to Christ, leaving all things behind so as to live obedience, poverty and chastity with Gospel simplicity, concrete signs of waiting for the Lord who comes without delay.

Porta Fidei, no. 13
October 11, 2011

91. *Christians*

By faith, across the centuries, men and women of all ages, whose names are written in the Book of Life (cf. Rev 7:9; 13:8), have confessed the beauty of following the Lord Jesus wherever they were called to bear witness to the fact that they were Christian: in the family, in the workplace, in public life, in the exercise of the charisms and ministries to which they were called.

Porta Fidei, no. 13
October 11, 2011

INDEX

*(Numbering refers to the sequential
positioning of each thought.)*